The Edge of Choice

Poetry on Mental Health

by Ludwig von Bewusstsein

The Edge of Choice

ISBN: 9781093547900 - provided by Amazon KDP.

Cover Photo provided by Photo by Daniel Olah on Unsplash

Cover Design by Ludwig Ompad - Canva and KDP Cover Creator

also by
Ludwig von Bewusstsein

Things That I Think I Intuitively Know
Volume I

Dedicated to

Those who opted out and
those who are still here,
fighting

Dear Reader,

     I imagine this book has come to your attention for serious reason. Perhaps you've been thinking about it, or know someone who is. Maybe you know someone whose committed the act, or perhaps you're just curious of another's neurosis in artistic form. Be it the former reasons, I sincerely hope the warrior within you is seeking companions in your war. That is, if you so desire company- if not, I'm sure it's within valid reason by your own standard and feelings that these moments should be a mission alone. Just know that by reading these words, I am a companion of yours forever in spirit. I've poured raw feelings of my experience into this book- and by doing so, it is my intention that you feel understood, heard, and accompanied.

     That being said, I must also note:

     Never let the fear that pervades these waters deter you from the presence of care. Be a seeker within this time, and always remember there are stars amongst the dark, cold space- resources available, one only needs to be resourceful, and reach. Be rich in your being, realizing value is everything.

In peace,

Ludwig von Bewusstsein

Table of Contents

and ever since
there's a part of me
that's often shocked mindful
          of the present
Ever since I almost took my own presence

-     LvB   " As Presence is Grim "

Then they say,
"I would never do that,
no matter what."

A pity that
your resilience
stifles imagination
starving empathy

- LvB   " Strength in its Blind Spots "

With every step
       I leave a step
              behind me

Being careful
       where I step
             is there a step
                    in front of me?

-     *LvB*   " *A Bridge is Only so Wide* "

Pardon me
there is rain
on my windshields

Tears blur the road
but sun shines fresh
after the fact

-   LvB   " Waiting it Out "

Comparing kills
when the critic
        strikes
in critical condition

-    LvB   " Hyper Critical Comparisons "

Perhaps if I weren't so sensitive
I would have never ended up
where death would entice

I contemplate the temptation
              jumping off, resignation
Choosing my final destination
              but I hear the shame
              shame
              on me
for feeling so much
that I can't shake it o f f

Back to contemplating
              jumping off

       -    LvB   " As Shame Cycles On "

*Sometimes depression feels like walking
hand-in-hand with death*

*How kind to keep me company
Inquiring if it's time
to cease my breath*

- *LvB*   " *Timing is Relevant, I suppose* "

Dance does me dandy
I move as it consumes me and
I feel alive-
then
one misstep, offbeat
a spiraling nosedive

The judgment I see and hear
how clothes dress
guilting myself
why I'm not at my best

Then, all of a sudden
I remember that view
how it looked ever steeper

-     LvB   " Your Own Blockade "

Lowly points of view make it hard to see
that anybody is truly there for me,
and even if friends are willing to listen,
I am not willing to trust

-    LvB   " Silence Weeps Loudly "

I still wake up
So I know my heart
    is still beating

Rhythm
    a little off beat
but still beating

-    LvB   " Though it is Faint "

If we all had theme music
    playing in the air
            Would we finally know
            sorrows we do not show?
                    Would we finally hear
                    what's been held back in fear?

-    LvB   " The Beauty Music Speaks "

There is a heavy gaze
through the mirror
that boldly proclaimed
love

The face settles tension
and I saw the shock in
my eyes

-     LvB   " Sad Surprise "

The energy that surrounds you
I can feel your contemplation
How to go about it,
        considering devastation

I acknowledge that consideration
Sincere thought since you would
        no longer be

Feeling like a ship stranded at sea
I can see winds look past your sails
You think it's time to bail, deciding
attempt must be met without fail

Sail still, my friend, there are still
        resources on this boat, and
There is goodness within you
        let it stay afloat

-    LvB   " Tidal Waves Greet You Hello "

Piano keys are often just black and white
yet don't they play a full harmonic scale?
The colors we see and all the gray in between
Portraying our emotions because it's harder
than it seems
Poetry like pianos, our words like keys
Writing, before life brings the poet
to their knees

-    LvB   " You Are Lock, Hole, and Key "

Discomfort likes to hold hands with ignorance
         and refer to their love as shame

The cruel? They're cruel
They think it's a game

Don't listen to these uneducated folk
Your feelings are not a fucking joke
If they really knew,
         they would choke
         on their own
         but stranger-friend
         you and me?
         we are not   alone
                   though   it feels l o n e l y

   -    LvB   " When Perspectives Fall Short "

The human
that is optimal you
sometimes   perhaps necessarily
you have to
suffer for it

-    LvB   " Delayed Shipping "

When rain falls harder
you can hear it on the ground
Sometimes I wonder
what I would have sounded like
        if I jumped
If I pitter-pattered, splattered
        on the ground

-    LvB   " Winter is Fitting "

It's comforting to know
there are keys and tones
that understand
what it feels like to be
alone

Channeling tears left
Waiting to drip
these melodies open
hope in despair

-    LvB   " The Magic of Pianos "

As dark clouds cover the sun
they cast out warmth and shine
        and I, the reason
why darkness has formed
causing water to storm
Forgive my absence of joy
I seem to have made a pact
with the eye of the storm

-    LvB   " When Blame Follows You Around "

All hearts matter
but that hardly matters
if you can't face personal matters

\-   *LvB*   " *Help Yourself Help Yourself, You Matter* "

The thing about energetic blocks
in loving, in believing, in trusting,
          and the like,
are that blocks have ninety-degree angles
Straight up, smooth, solid surface
          No way to hinge a climb
          You either bust through
          or jump high enough
                    in time

-     LvB   " No Way Around Blocks "

"You're supposed to be joyous this season."
I know, but I'm not
in season

-    *LvB*   " *Holiday Cheer* "

and for some of us
        Depression
is a fast track to
        Spirituality

      with tiny sinkholes
      that make your tires
         Bop
      and your sad face
         Cringe

-    LvB   " Oooof, My Vehicle Felt That One "

What a way to spend
insomnia
Laying down, turned to the side
Breaking down, bawling, but
all it really looks like
is blank staring into nothing
as darkness grins back
a familiar assassin attacks

-    LvB   " Bedtime Routines "

No one feels comfortable speaking
about their suicidal thoughts
because once uttered out loud
you tend to hear invalidation
       and all that does is
       add to the shock
That's already there, the shock
       when you noticed
       you're really
       considering

Don't they get it?
Judgemental energy is fucking
       inhibiting

-     LvB   " Inexperienced Without a Clue "

I imagine you break your own heart
Catching feelings for someone, but
feeling like you're no longer lovable
Hopes up just to feel your chest drop
This is what it's like to crush on someone
when you have depression, using repression
emotions engulf you

Just needing someone to hold you
or at least your hand or your heart
Thinking you're smart, you break down
how you can't be loved
Nor could you bring love to the table
but I think, you can love yourself
being mind and heart stable
In such a place surely you'll be able
to erupt your dormant love
despite all your labels

-    LvB   " Hopeful Romantic, Lover of Self "

I suppose there is
beauty in depression,   e x p a n d e d
        compassion to those
        who I once thought
        I understood

-    LvB   " To Think So Before You Experience So "

Depression is something that I thought I once knew
but being depressed gives you a new point of view
See, you look for cues, news to justify your suicide
while looking for ways to renew inside, and if not
  you hope you get caught
  in the crossfire of some tragedy-
    see?
We may be depressed but we have strategy
  but maybe, with the wrong goals

-    LvB   " To Consider the End or End-Goal "

28

I just want to age with a smile
            on my face
and that's not going to happen
            by saving face

        -    LvB   " Yet I Still Hesitate "

Shout out to all the friends
who lift you up when you're feeling down
and shame on those who make you feel like
it's not okay to frown
Tsk tsk, don't they know that one would drown
if feelings aren't fully felt safe and sound?

but still, we spare the inexperienced
and appreciate companion coherence
for those who know, are considerate
in soul

- LvB   " Smiles in Muddy Common Ground "

The thing about feeling overwhelmed is that
you feel like you're at the helm of a ship
          that's been sunken down,
Struck by unforeseen torpedoes in turbulent waters
It's all a fight, the fright that you're going to
drown while witnessing the beauty of ocean reef
          all around,
What will it take to get back above and on
          solid, stable ground?

A wholesome being must be found,
staying afloat in the here and now

    -    LvB   " Overencumbered Vessel "

I'm either going
to bloom
or wilt

-   *LvB*   " *Poppy Season* "

In these dreary moments
the wonder seems to be
        To become empowered
        or
        To drown at sea

        Is it not?
                To persevere
                or
                To opt out

-    LvB   " Contemplating with the Lights Off "

and ever since
I contemplated
at the edge
of that nocturnal bridge
The view, my outlook
has never been
the same

An underlying image
that one day, one scene
will abruptly conclude
this motion picture
This motion of turbulence

\-   LvB   " When Suicide Haunts "

When I feel alone I look around me
No one, no thing, can ground me
As I stand drowning
        words erupt, and
        poetry surrounds me
Such a craft
a beauty
Even hand and paper
        find a bond
Letting ink play and
        remind me
that I am never alone
I am beauty inside me

   -    LvB   " Our Light Gleaming its Infinite Charge "

Something within
me, that does not want me
to speak, it sees this ink and
words jotted with meaning-
too weak
You lack this and that, but
I know it's face
I have seen him around

From my feet that dance a joyous step
to my anticipating left hand
that ignites poetry through pen on paper-
you have followed me
Why am I haunting me?

-    LvB   " Watch Out, The Self-Critic is a Stalker "

The anticipation of leaving, lingering
An aversion catching my attention
Like wind catching my sails
          Shall I voyage on
          or withdraw
or should I just abandon ship?

Shooting from the hip in the dark
Do I even know what I'm aiming for?

    -    LvB   " When Direction is Useless "

Cold winds comfort the heated summer
As the sun sets, darkness caves into
the night
Stars visible, but with cold distance

Fire that does not warm nor burn
Letting its light be offered

-   LvB   " Conditions Just Right to be Alright "

Ludwig used Self-Destruct!
. . .   But it failed!

    -    LvB   " Phew, No Save Points Here "

In search for a Silver Key
We default for a Silver Bullet

\-   *LvB*   " *Treasure is Priceless to a Dead Man* "

Maybe some suicides were answering
        calls to action
because all you gave was a reaction
        "That's the easy way out"
        "That's selfish to do"
        "There are people who have it worse than you"

        We know that
minus points of worth
in the negative now
Committing to death
        with a vow

-     LvB   " Silence Listens Well "

Sometimes, when I hear you speak
I listen in closely and hear trembling
knees

Communication weeps the stories
we can hardly bear to speak

\-   LvB   " Channels in Which we Grieve "

How exciting, all giddy and strong
When in the midst of feeling like
　　　　　you don't belong
You see your best self is yet to come

-　　　LvB　　　" Mighty in Heart "

I remember I used to say,
"Those who underestimate
love,
underestimate themselves."

No wonder I can't sum
the value of my being

- *LvB*   " *Irony in Retrospect* "

If I hadn't told myself
prior to that ring

"No matter what, you're going to live."

It would have been a call-
a life
short-lived, indeed

\-   LvB   " Self-Saving-Talk "

Motivation has a motor
and the fuel burns on hope
It is the precursor to believing
you can uphill this slope

-   *LvB*   " *Hope Efficiently* "

If this is it, and I have too much choice
This lack of ammo suffices so I can blow my brains out with no noise

   Then the sun rises and I have to return to poise

- LvB " Silencer "

Crashing against the shores
waves roar
Greeting noise, sharp
like the sudden touch
of ice

The deep blue in ocean flow
illuminated from
a luminescent moon of silver-white glow

A beautiful moment to know
Deciding here I must grow

Shining, shrouded, surrounded in darkness
Yet blood activated and now it glows
It is warmth beating in my heart
Thawing internal blistering snow

Melting all into the ocean
as one processes emotions
Knowing to heal is devotion

- LvB " Moments you Know "

Be honest if you use suppression
Be honest about your depression
Be honest with yourself
Feeling known should be validated through yourself

Be honest, you're not alone
It's just quiet space
            between us
It just seems lonely
            is all

  -    LvB   " Honest Mirrors Crack Your Views "

Love phases through us in all kinds of ways
Terribly, if you have to ask yourself or say
        when someone likes you
        "Am I worth some pain?"
Knowing me- all these issues and walls
The path to me is a long, winding hall
        with trap tiles and doors
The ability to earthquake it all to the ground
        without a sound
I could be gone, am I worth knowing-
To see the instability, you would never fall in love
but I want you to like me, and I want to be in love

Time just hasn't shown me if I can balance
        that, and self-love
I can't risk rooting myself only for a lover
        to uproot who
        I am becoming

-    LvB   " Can You Love What's Reviving but Ill? "

I consume a red and white-dotted mushroom
Doot-doot-doot- an enlarged, expanded view

\-   *LvB*   " *Mario's Holistic Secrets* "

Well-intentioned, but short-sighted view
        of elders to point out our youth
        as if mirrors don't tell
We know, but we're living in hell

"I'm depressed," said the youth
"But you're so young! You have your whole life ahead of you!"
        said the elder
Silence ensues as youth thinks about truth and age

but youth and gratitude
does not guarantee joy
as shame thinks it a ploy
        and now
        we're realizing, self-worth does not bloom
        from youthful skin, but from deep within

    -    LvB   " Age in its Validation "

It just fucking sucks to realize
        if I could easily afford
            a gun
I would have blasted myself
        by now

That instant act saves a trip
        back to the bridge
        with second thoughts

On second thought-
                I'm going to outlive suicidal thoughts

    -    LvB   " Indecisive Seconds "

Trauma leaves a bitter taste like
a cringe-worthy flavor that memory won't erase
a palate that can smell its presence-
it's putrid
yet its influence is elusive
Subtly polarizing you nonconducive-
the truth is, now?
Now that you're aware
when trauma shows itself, you can just stare
face to face with frequent fears

Being with it now, you're all ears
No more running from a reservoir of tears
Draining eyes into wisdom is releasing beasts that sneer

You hear them faintly
Lessons they had to convey
as you wave them goodbye
and greet the new day

-    LvB   " The Trauma That Taught "

When the night shows and rain settles in
We nest in shadows seeking shelter and rest
       but the moon conjures trauma
       and demons pull the sheets
       sacrificing sleep
Don't turn on the lights so soon
Sometimes you need to let your emotions   sway and swoon
Letting the night take its course
       as water is to moon

-     LvB   " Tossing and Turning with Purpose "

I looooooooove chillin'
especially at the edge
The tippy turn straight down
at the apex of a bridge

\-   *LvB*   " *When the Mood is Just Wrong* "

I've noticed something, saddening,   sadly
        Stigmas shame the status enough
so when you diagnose you put on a smile and hope nobody calls
your bluff-
If they call you out, you'll just nod and fall out
All alone with no one to talk to even with a phone or someone
right beside you or even in the mirror, inside you
        Solemnly saddening, social setting
            still smiling and laughing
                Knowing when you're alone
                it's called surviving

-    LvB   " Notifications "

Frightening-
how subtle the presence
depression
has
as
suicidal thoughts
don't knock at all
or even wait for a call
persistently inviting to fall

-    LvB   " Unresponsive Invitations "

Genuine kindness has sharp edges-
        if they've got nothing nice to say
        they can kindly fuck off
        with their bullshit state of mind
as we renovate and protect our energetic boundaries
        over time

   -    LvB   " Enduring the Desensitized "

Tears shed within this hollow tree
like sap slowly drips on the trunk
though I am in a funk
I will keep growing
for I am a tree
in a forest, yet lone
I will not fall, but will make a sound
as I dig my roots deep into the ground
branching out a voice
bearing fruit by choice

- LvB "Fruition"

Sleeping states essential
as the depressed only get
       two to three
Smashing in waves
I wish I could go down under
       with the current
       back into the sea
Teaching me how to let it go
Washing me ashore
Attempting sleep once more

-    LvB   " Early-Morning-Dreary "

Living in a state of lack
I feel as if the universe has borders
Trapped by emotions, they give me orders
I cannot choose to ignore

-    LvB   " Slave to the State of Mind "

When you feel alone
Put down your phone
Stand in the darkness you may know
Light a candle as they say
Illuminate yourself to be okay
Okay that you're alone, but no longer   lonely

   -    LvB   " Scrolling isn't Healing "

Turbulence has a sound
Critical snares heard in silence

"Nobody will care about your poetry"
"You look stupid when you dance"
"You're just a depressed fool"
"Nobody would love you"
"You're not enough"
- but, I am

I am enough
I love myself
I'm healing
I'm flowing
I'm in awe

-    LvB   " Clouds Drift as Turbulence Passes "

silence
amongst
resilience

.   .   .   .

celebration
appreciation   none of it
                      fucking acknowledge me!

        -     LvB   " Cried Oneself Grateful "

Sometimes I forget what it feels like
to live without seeing Death's appeal

- *LvB* " *Sunset Colors* "

When I see the act
of love between two
a jealous depression
s
i
n
k
s
　　　　me
Realization of trauma
to be romantic once more
Drowning but ashore
Even on the good days
the waves still ebb and flow
as love demands to l e t g o

-    LvB   " The Anchor is Stuck "

Misaligned actions
bring death to intentions
as foreshadow is cast

-    *LvB*   " *Suicide Prevention Day* "

A pity to be bound
by a bond with links of words
that make me feel pathetic
I can't break what's been heard

-    LvB   " Words Ring "

As the mirror witnesses
the eyes reflect what we feel
but cannot see
and if the mirror could
surely it would weep

-   LvB   " Eyes Remember You "

A sour mind cannot taste the sweetness
of our hearts

-     *LvB*   " *Natural Flavors, No Sugar Added* "

Relapsing addict
Impulsivity to death
Killing one's own voice

\-   LvB   " Addictions Write Haikus "

As night fades away to welcome the day
Kindly, the gradient of the sky greets us to awake

Like morning dew drips from the flower
We depart from the beauty of ease
The beauty of restful sleep

-   LvB   " Good-good Mornings for You "

and however you choose to have me
I will make your mind race, busy-fast-pace
so you don't go to that place

-    LvB   " Fresh Coffee and Tasks Don't Last "

As the night fades into the sky
A calming tone starts to follow
Quieting the city lights, and
             turning off minds

-    *LvB*   " *Rejuvenating Nights* "

Addictions are jars of water and oil
intentions and actions
as these two fail to mix
I separate into growth and quick fix
I am not one, but two, I am split
I wish to be whole, yet I do not quit
Figuring out a way to bust open the lid
Pouring myself out, discipline past doubt

-     LvB   " Jars Shatter with Enough Impact "

Emotions are only overwhelming
when you neglect discharge
The human canvas is expansive enough
          to hold all the colors of emotion
Yet you think you have none, though you are
          the brush, and paint-

                                        paint
                                        paint

-    LvB   " One Canvas Renews "

Thoughts needn't be followed
off the cliff
or a bridge-
any drop that would do
any action that would
eliminate you

- LvB   " Thoughts (not) as Actions "

Like a character who hasn't learned
their best move-
yet

-     LvB   " Special Skills for Every Class "

Insecurities
are bred
by a society that feeds you
garbage

malnutrition

malevolence

Time reveals the choice
to be made
feeding yourself
mental, physical, spiritual
first aid

-    LvB   " Nutritional Facts "

The sun thaws
a frozen, traumatized
      heart
      just right
Dancing in the sunlight
Letting sorrows play their tune

-    LvB   " Conditions and Gratitude "

Did you know that even diamonds and pearls
have their imperfections?
Yet, their magnificence is still revered

\-   *LvB*   " *Humans in the Right Light* "

If you were lonely for too long
would you accompany yourself before it's too late?
          Perhaps
you view yourself with hate
and that's why loneliness kills

-    LvB   " No One to Stop Thought but You "

Love, changes you
Attention to, changes you

\-   *LvB*   " *Give Yourself Attention* "

Depression is grief, trapped in our body
Unable to find a path to express
Light, in its absence,   repress

Depression is a bad connection, with self
Troubleshooting reception   failed
No signal, try again?   Retry
                               Retry

-     LvB   " As Many Times Needed is the Charm "

A lethal grip
that slows life to a picture
as timeframes pass by

"Let me go, please, I want to live in the moment"

"I cannot," said the addiction
"You have taken time for granted,
you have chosen to spend it with me."

As addiction sees me off
I head toward constant destinations
to be present, and free

-    LvB   " Impulses and Choice "

Depression alarms my internal state
as sirens howl through the skies
an emergency is underway

As clouds dim the day
Borders like early fate
Taking one's life with hate

-    LvB   " The Alarm and its Purpose "

As piano keys play a melody to soothe
Tsunamis to a calm, heart in palm-
Even a piano does not have the key
to put my beating treasure
back in my chest

-    LvB   " Treasures of No Key "

Why deny that sometimes you need to frown-
　　　that sometimes you need to settle down
　　　and let the colors fade into the background

True appreciation when it's time to rise
Coloring in and seeing a masterpiece-
　　　yourself a prize

-　　LvB　　" Golden Sunsets and Rise "

It's always the next day, tomorrow is it
then time comes to pass and you pass by it
another step forward shy
was self esteem is still shaken by the earthquakes in you
on and on, seismic chaos continues to ensue
until one day it breaks the surface
The crust that hides a desolate, hollowed being
you're exposed, an abomination-
Light graces you and begins a transformation
a deeper knowing of your nature
the sun, sky, ocean, and the bay
What of these natures are elements we convey?

-     LvB   " Scenery in its Phases "

I care   but I don't
I care   but I don't

-    *LvB*   " *Perfectly Indecisive Imbalance* "

A seed does not think it a flower, it knows it must sprout
It is an effort and a knowing that this is a soiled, aligned
route
Up, and through, blooming to an open sky
Clouds pass as the wind howls through the crevice
of a canyon that was a shell of you
Transformation introduces the wind to greet the flower
that is you

\-   LvB   " Built to be Buried then Bloom "

If there is a light that leads me to my end
       I would close my eyes and pretend
That my whole life wasn't already a lonesome tunnel
       from the beginning with no light
I would fail to resist and I would run toward the birthing rays
       and the tunnel would get smaller and smaller
       I would squeeze out the end in a cartoonish manner
What the hell was all of that if your show didn't matter   ?

-    LvB   " Fall in Love with your Character "

Livelihood is sure
to come alive
someday
and with it
Fulfillment, surely

-    LvB   " Grit's Grace "

Broken hearts   broken hearts
Beats that are quiet yet the emotions run deep
        uncharted depth
To resurface is unknown   sinking
        ever more, buoyant like
                a stone
Mirror reflections of someone I had known
Mistakes committed that I do not condone
        self-prescribing fate to be alone
        It's truly weird . . .
Perpetuation of that which we feared
        abuse, violence
        wishing for some
        silence, yet
We can't give a moment to ourselves
Inmates, to our own prison cells
Pleading for a pardon from your
        heart that's hardened
unknown   a broken heart is a garden
        soil rich
        to grow
Time and nourishment, factors that will show
it does not happen overnight, victorious
        internal fight

    -    LvB   " Resuscitation and Calm Breathing "

Shedding ego   letting self go
Titles that which we identify
One cannot simply simplify the experience that is
            do who inside
An identity crisis, no matter the age, doesn't set up the stage-
            stage-fright   nothing looks right
            body feels tight   you're tense
Perhaps it's because we've been living in past tense . . .

stage-fright, "what if I don't burn bright?"
nothing looks right, yet you've never been to this height
body feels tight, uncomfortable, not quite
realizing that your heart feels light
            in present tense

Finally honoring who you are and the footsteps in the dirt,
through the mud, on a fine sand beach, and all that your being
could reach
Ambitious, because you set the bar   grateful for your grit
            to venture this far

    -    LvB   " Onward Words "

Dramas   dramatic   when you live life on
automatic
you might forget to shift gears, especially when it comes time to
downshift
shedding tears
f e e l i n g all these fears, afraid of reaching ears
gossip
          it goes behind us all, when in truth, all humans fall
          remembering your spirit
          is immeasurable

no longer suicidal
beating hearts, your pulse is vital
the picture isn't as big without you
so stare back boldly in that mirror
and lock eyes with your compassion

    -    LvB   " Semi-Automatic Emotion Machines "

Untamed and unknown
Sides to yourself you hadn't known
Wondering who you are, feeling alone
Failing to acknowledge how much you've really grown
Holding it together, hoping nobody sees
This broken person that wishes to be free
       from their own sharp edges
Yet when opportunities are presented, an often flee
Powerless, it seems, yet we are the ones who deem
       imploding or healthy self-esteem
External situations, indeed they matter
but realize the power of inner chatter
       it's how you estrange yourself
       it's how you take care
It's the reason the mirror gives an impolite glare
       so when things don't seem fair
Connect with yourself, let yourself share
       it is our burdened gift to bare
       our potential
       if we so dare

-    LvB   " Endless Discoveries in Self-Awareness "

I never would have thought a mirror would hear me
           asking myself if we're here to stay

There's still more to your story   yet to be told
           honor that, and
           let it unfold

    -     LvB   " So Dual Voices Say "

Addiction swallows me whole, as impulsive actions take hold
This lack of self-control is an itch I cannot reach-
A lesson here, the universe will teach
how to unshackle my ankles and wrists
yet I seem to follow pain, a masochistic choice in vain
self-infliction, self-worth
If only I could see the beauty, like I do mother earth
I'd be able to lift myself up to the heavens above
Embody the lessons and light that is self-love

-     LvB   " A Fighter's Haven "

Roses, now, are blood red and violets are bleak and blue
When I was younger, I didn't have a clue
Unaware of what life could have in store
                at least for me-
suicidal thoughts and suffering throughout my core
being, doing, living, the most dreadful chores
but like the red roses and blue violets
these states we identify with come to pass
Only when we appreciate the way in which we bloom
                can we say "at last"
So acknowledge yourself, don't leave that a task for
                someone else
Embody the power of your voice and catch yourself
                before you jump
                consider your choice
Choosing self-transformation, making beauty out of frustration
                self-innovation, a more refined illustration

  -    LvB   " Masterpiece Out of You "

I imagine it must be rough, trying to forgive yourself is tough
Ridden with guilt, the actions uncut, emotions to evade
Living behind a mask and under the rug
where we rarely sweep and demons eat, shit, and sleep
Empathy cleans the reflection well and inside the mirror
you dwell, you weep, you toss and turn in your sleep
Another day lived with courage into the night
The bravest act of all
An emotionally-informed decision
To live on, with intention, action with precision

-    LvB   " The Subtle Deal that is to Heal "

Careful to forsake
Self talk stirs in you
      a conversation
      taken for granted

-    *LvB*   " *Self-Loather* "

When we wake from dreams
to the pursuit of
We are engined to burn coal
To exert energy   despite   it   a l l
and as we combust   through it   all
Overwhelming sensations nod one off to a rugged nap
Where do I find more coal?
Are there any other fuels?
Is it in the food that should nourish me?

or

Is it in the water that hydrates a parched heart?

Blinded by depths that sun does not breach
It burns, and I see   I feel
Resourcefulness beyond fuel, resilience
as inspired emotions propel perseverance

-    LvB   " On Some Days "

You have let yourself in but you stand by the door
            obnoxiously knocking
As if you haven't already intruded once more
The bullet to a gun, the impulse of addiction
Sent to kill me once again   yet
            the safety is on
I am aware of your presence   thank you for knocking
As I leave you to a honeymoon
within the present moment
We create a new space, and if you come knocking there
We'll find a new place and move and move again and again
and if you still intrude, and our fate is a never-ending feud
I will be still, yet go beyond time and space to arrive at no place
                                    a target you cannot

chase

    -    LvB   " Evasive Maneuvers "

as if emotions need an appeal
yet we play our own judge
and I'm guilty as charged

-    LvB   " Invalidation and Sentences "

Light seeps through the cloud
Only to shine what is blue
The ocean in you

-    LvB   haiku on emotions and mindset

Prison mind of painful memories of past times
      as if to remind horrid actions
          of mine
Reactions to this, unjustified, yet poorly proposed
as the subconscious impairs conscious intention
Lessons that need attention
      discomfort and
      difficult retention
      I sit in meditation
          I change my relation
          graced a serene elation
          in contemplation
          an equanimous revelation
Simply a complex situation shining light on our subconscious
      freeze, fight, or flight-
Conscious now of our ways, forever changed are how we live
          our days

-    LvB   " Self-Sentenced "

A bridge hangs over a busy harbor
        for over passing vehicle use
I use the midpoint edge, hanging
            looking over the edge
            on a nights harbor
            as I find my point
                to be

    -    LvB   " 3am Contemplations and Different Use "

Guilty has me full
Leaking drips until my death
Emptied self respect

-    LvB   haiku on guilt

I fight the new drug
To honor and love myself
Discipline of mind

- *LvB*   *haiku inspired by Fight The New Drug*

Beautiful, breathing, breathtaking park
Grant me peace
Outdoors   turmoils cease

-    LvB   " Reconnecting in Nature "

Like light, breaking through the clouds
          shimmering on the ocean
I contemplate emotions that run deep
          like this Pacific blue sea
When you look inside yourself, what do you see?
Face to face with adversity, we may choose to flee
Each of us choosing our own dismantling ecstasy-
          That is to say, rather, we drown
To the darkest depths of the ocean, unmet by light
          starting to lose sight
          but when we choose to ignite
Inner light, we may be surprised at what we find
          the forgotten   the unknown
A hardened heart, more solid than stone
          but like the light reflecting off the ocean
          if we shed light on our emotions, reflect
          to remember erosion, and how it softens
          hearts to a colorful, deserted beach
For us to frolic, right beyond depressions reach

-     LvB   " The Breath of Ebb and Flow "

It is the battle within
as much as the wars
we wage

For peace only starts
with you, and you
on the same
page

\-   LvB   " Moments Blank Page "

In a sea of people
you can't help but wonder
      if you'll drown
Pulling yourself deep under or
      if you'll break the surface
      gasping for air
with someone there throwing you a tube
                a buoy
        a helping hand
that helps you understand you
      can stay afloat-
      you take note
You have to tread and keep your head above water
but sometimes you can be still and float
a calm breathing presence like an anchored boat

-    LvB   " Help Yourself to Fresh Air "

The flavors of our tears
do not complement
gravity
and gravity
does not ground
our sorrows and fears
yet
it is through our suffering does wisdom hear
and we learn to hold love dear

-    LvB   " Complementary Ingredients are Key "

Although this is the end
        there still lies a twist
                this book may close
                        our stories will end
                                but today we live on
                                        my warrior friend

                                Begin
                                        Begin
                                Begin

    -    LvB   " Creator's Fortune "

Author's Note:

Writing this collection was ultimately a healing process for me. It was a project that I knew had to express, but at times, I was worried that I was perpetuating my depression and suicidal thoughts by giving them the attention and effort to articulate them. Externalizing my thoughts was a challenge, but it was necessary to help me move forward. So I approached the creation of this book slowly, and didn't try to force any writing. The poetry is present, raw words as I felt the emotions. It felt gruesome, yet liberating.

I believe words can change the world, and if my words helped change your vicious, internal world, then I am honored to have taken duty in your fight.

Lastly, I just want to mention (and disclose) that this is no substitute for mental health care. Instead, I hope this book to be a part of your accumulative catalyst that enacts you to seek help. Being resourceful is a choice away, and I know it's hard, but we're in this together... and

WE GOT THIS - keep in touch:
Instagram: @vonbewusstsein
Website: www.vonbewusstsein.com

In peace,

Ludwig von Bewusstsein

About the Author:

With a name translating to "Famous Warrior of Consciousness"- Filipino American Poet Ludwig von Bewusstsein is on a mission to bring more conscious awareness to the subconscious mind. Through his poetry, Ludwig aspires to invoke wonder and integration in each reader. His greatest ambition is for his art to positively influence the emergent properties of society by helping the individual gain a more profound perception of life.

Ludwig's first experience with poetry was in Jr. High School. Exploring the subject as a class, they were assigned a project to create a 15-page poetry book. As much as he enjoyed the project, he didn't think much about pursuing poetry after the class moved on to another subject matter.

At the age of 25, a quarter-life crisis ended up being the catalyst to rediscover himself through poetry. Exploring genres such as Existential, Love, and Mental Health- he continues to learn the craft of poetry by studying, reading, and writing it. Although new to the poetry scene, Ludwig is simply grateful that poetry itself has welcomed him with open arms.

Made in the USA
Coppell, TX
01 August 2021